Praise for
Fearless Communication
and Dave Tester

"Dave's principles have made the difference between being a major league technology services company versus being a minor league company. Bringing in Dave has been one of the best things that we have done as a business. You have to have a system to get five-star Google reviews and the *Fearless Communication* system works."

—Tom Beeles, President and CEO,
Allied Business Solutions

"I've worked with Dave on over 6,000 customer calls. We have gained invaluable feedback and improved customer relationships with the Director of First Impressions."

—Deborah Flagan, Vice President, Hayden Homes

"Dave's system has increased our overall Google review star rating which is extremely important in today's society. Upset customers post reviews without being asked but happy customers won't unless you ask. He has taught us how to ask the happy customers for reviews and reach out to unhappy customers to resolve their concerns."

—Jeff Cox, owner, Right Now Heating
and Air Conditioning

"Dave Tester is a genius at what he does. He has worked with my clients and team for years, and I can attest that his program works. His method will take pressure off of your team, provide results (our appointments increased by over 35%), and make your marketing ROI shoot through the roof."

—Shaun Buck, CEO, The Newsletter Pro

"Hands down, the best method to book appointments and increase revenue. My clinic has used Dave's system for a year, and the revenue difference is astounding. Using the *Fearless Communication* system is a no-brainer—read and implement this system, and your business will flourish."

**—Dr. Derrick Nelson, owner,
Town & Country Veterinary Clinic**

"My firm and my team are forever grateful for Dave's efforts and time with us. Utilizing the voicemail conundrum and the 'I miss you letter' have proven to be two of our biggest strategies. In the six years Dave has worked with our team, sales have increased over 200%. His ability to adapt his training to each team member's needs was an overwhelming success. I recommend Dave and his team 100%."

**—Chris Spates, co-founder and managing partner,
Benefit Bank Distributors, Inc.**

How to Energize Your Team
for Success on the Phone

FEARLESS
COMMUNICATION

Dave
Tester

Fearless Communication
How to Energize Your Team for Success on the Phone
By Dave Tester © 2020

Softcover ISBN: 978-1-61206-207-5
eBook ISBN: 978-1-61206-208-2
PDF eBook ISBN: 978-1-61206-218-1

For more information, visit GoDaveTester.com

To purchase this book at quantity discounts, contact Aloha Publishing at alohapublishing@gmail.com.

Published by

ALOHA
PUBLISHING

Printed in the United States of America

For the original Testers:

My grandpa, David O.

My dad, Dr. Tester

My uncles, Bob and Jon

In some way you all have mentored me through great times and challenging ones. I am blessed because of your touch in my life and this book.

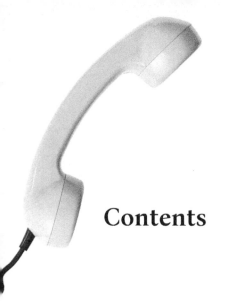

Contents

I hope the pages that follow will assist you and
your team in finding success through
Fearless Communication.

Dave

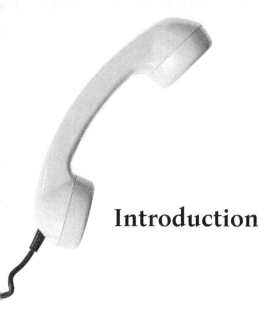

Introduction

Being listened to and being loved are so similar that most of your customers and prospects would not be able to tell you the difference between the two. This resource in your hands is key for any business owner or staff member who has people picking up the phone regularly.

Despite what some people may think, the phone is far from dead in 2020. In fact, according to *Wired* magazine, 162 billion inbound phone calls were made in 2019 alone. Remote workforces are increasing, and the phone is as important as ever to stay connected. If that doesn't get your attention, maybe this will—when your phone rings, the client on the other end *wants to buy*. Do yourself and your business a favor by booking an appointment the proper way.

My scripts will help you accomplish that very thing. Stop educating your customers and use the phone to give people the help they actually need. The tools included in this book will help you capitalize on clues like tone and tempo, which comprise an astounding 93 percent of communication over the phone. Believe it or not, only seven percent of your communication is made up by the spoken word. Our hope is that your motto will become "Listen with intent to understand" rather than "Listen with intent to respond." This book will help you comprehend the vast difference between the two.

Your team members on the front line speak to 99 percent of your clients and prospects on the phone. That same staff, on average, gets less than two percent of the training offered in your company. Reading this book is the first step to changing that dismal statistic. If you are interested in ensuring that your customers keep coming back and your prospects continue to make appointments, this book is a fantastic start.

As I travel this great country of ours training and coaching teams to achieve success, I hear many business leaders express the same frustration. "I pay good money to provide my staff with the tools and the training that they need for success, but they continue to do it their own way." While I may not feel your pain as a business owner, I do understand it. This book will finally make it fun for your team to win on the phone. Better yet, it will stop leads from walking out your door and customers from leaving your business because they don't feel valued.

The first step is easy. We're going to ask your team to slow down on the phone, listen, and take notes. Learning to demonstrate empathy and following my scripts makes it easy for your team members to win.

The average M.D. starts out with $200,000 in school debt and about half a million dollars in expenses to launch a small practice. The average attorney will spend, counting law school, $350,000 to $1 million to launch a practice. Your business may be similar in nature or one that is completely different in scope. It doesn't really matter. Our tools have helped copy and print companies, HVAC and plumbing companies, automotive companies, veterinary clinics, dentist offices, and so many more businesses.

Money is leaking out of your business in the form of lost leads and customers. What's the point of investing thousands of dollars to build a business if your front desk team loses customers at hello? Don't you think it's time to patch the leaky bucket? Don't let your leads and customers run away.

As a teenager, I worked on a ranch, where I had to haul water in two five-gallon buckets. One day, someone had taken my good watering buckets, so I found two other buckets. They were rusted and I think one was used for target practice with a pellet gun. As a stubborn 15-year-old, I thought I could fill up the buckets and run to the water trough before much would leak out. But no matter how fast I ran, they would nearly run dry before I reached the trough.

Leaky buckets won't hold water no matter how hard you work.

Like most business owners, you may spend many dollars on lead generation. Your goal is to fill your bucket with leads. The challenge is your lead bucket has holes in it—not from rust, but from your staff who work the phones. Many people are spending more money than ever to try to fill the proverbial bucket with leads and customers, using tools like Google, SEO, radio, TV, books, Facebook, LinkedIn, and more. Whatever we're told the latest and greatest trend is, we'll try it, all with the hope of landing a lead. But they tend to spend very little on training the person whose job it is to take those leads and turn them into customers. The truth is the leads are solid and the water in the bucket is good, but the problem lies in the bottom of the bucket. Until we fix those holes, we'll continue to leak lost leads and customers. We simply *must* teach our teams how to answer the phone.

Far too many customers, leads, and prospects are draining out the holes in the bottom of your bucket. Let's fix the leaky bucket.

You have a choice. You can kick the bucket and pray that it gets better, or even yell and scream at your team to do it. But why not choose a better way? Implement the tools in this book and patch up those holes in the leaky bucket forever.

I look forward to helping you on your journey.

1

The Platinum Rule: Treat Others How They Want to Be Treated

I learned an important lesson in the sixth grade. Dalton Gardens Elementary was my school, but my education came from 5801 Colfax Street. That was our house. Dr. Tester, a veterinarian, was my dad. Our house on Colfax Street doubled as a veterinary clinic early in his career.

A telephone with a push-button dial sat in the dining room on a desk that served as a divider between my mom's great cooking in the kitchen and the living room. It had a wire connected to the wall and a very loud ring. The way it sat on that desk, visitors got the feeling they were walking up to a makeshift front desk. You know, the kind of front desk that serves as the gateway in a business.

That phone rang all the time, or so it seemed. Sometimes it was friends or family, but mostly it was clients looking for help to solve the sickness of their dogs, cats, horses, and cows at all hours of the day and night. When my dad was making house calls, I answered the phone. I was a sixth grader learning the art of customer care, and I must say it wasn't art at first. In fact, it was often a complete mess.

My dad would come home and ask about the calls he had missed. "Who called while I was gone? What was their name, and did you get a phone number?"

Heck, all I cared about was getting back outside to play football with my neighbor, Ed Benson. The phone was a distraction, even a bother. I said vaguely, "Someone called about a sick horse. They said they'd call back later."

But my dad wanted to know *all* of the details. "Where do they live? Did they sound worried or concerned?" He even asked if I knew the horse's name.

"Pop, I don't remember. That was a whole hour ago. I'm pretty sure it was a brown horse. I'm sure they'll call back. Can I go back outside now?"

"Sure, but not before you learn how we answer the phone."

If only I had known back then that this was the beginning of my training that would lead me to gain the title Director of First Impressions—I would have at least pretended to be enthusiastic.

As an entrepreneur or businessperson, it's important to remember that the phone ringing is never a distraction. It's how we put food on the table. Dad used to say, "Nothing happens until a sale is made." I can still hear him reminding me of the importance of the client and how we needed to take care of them, even on the phone, if I wanted to have money for new football cleats.

"Please don't let it ring more than three times," Dr. Tester loved to remind me.

"How come, Dad? If they want you bad enough, won't they wait for an answer?"

"No." In fact, Dad told me that after three rings they would call another veterinarian and that would be the end of the relationship or something he called a "lead." Dad added this question to the three-ring rule: "You do like to eat, don't you, son?"

The learning never seemed to stop with Dr. Tester. Dad asked me to get a first name, a last name, and a phone number.

My dad told me that the client—what he called a "prospect"—would be impressed that we cared enough to get a first and last name and used their name while we were talking with them on the phone.

"Please ask for their name and how to spell it. And most importantly, always—and I mean *always*—get a phone number."

The next day after school, I was almost excited to get a phone call and try out the homework my dad had given me. Later, Dad asked me about the calls as he walked through the front door.

"Dad, Willard Sheets called—772-2601—and I answered on the second ring!"

I had done my job perfectly, or so I thought.

My dad asked, "What did he want? How did he sound? Was he worried or upset? Was it the horse or that new dog?"

"You never told me I needed all of that."

Dalton Gardens Grade School was for math and history, but Colfax Street was for a lifetime of customer care and answering the phone correctly.

I picked it up eventually—names, numbers, dog, cat, horse, happy, sad, and upset. "Is this an emergency?" "How do we find your house?"

Although I didn't realize it, I had become the Director of First Impressions for the family practice. All I needed to know to answer the phone like a professional I learned as a sixth grader under the tutelage of my dad.

This chapter alone can change the cash flow of your business immediately. It's the first step to mending your leaky bucket. Write down how much you spend on marketing to make your phone ring, and then figure out what it costs per hour to keep your business running. You need to know the numbers: the cost of a lost lead and the cost to make the phone ring.

When it rings, answer it like a pro—the way Dr. Tester would want you to answer it. Remember to always answer before the third ring.

I prescribe this opening line for all inbound calls: "It's a great day at [your business]! This is Dave [the name of your Director of First Impressions]! How can I help you?"

The reason behind how we answer the phone is twofold.

First, it allows us to take control of the call. No matter what the caller says after that script, we always reply first with, "Absolutely. Real quick, remind me of your first name."

The second reason is that it gives you a chance to determine how the person on the other end of the line wants to be communicated with. Here is where the title of this chapter, "The Platinum Rule," comes into play. I love the golden rule: Treat others how you want to be treated. On the phone, however, the platinum rule says to treat others how *they* want to be treated.

After you say with enthusiasm, "It's a great day at our business! This is _____ speaking! How may I help you?" The prospect will reply in one of four ways, depending on their DISC personality type.

A Dominant type will say, "This is Dave. My horse is sick. Can you help me?" Based on DISC training, a Dominant needs to win, and they have a fear of being taken advantage of. Speak up and say, "Dave, absolutely. Real quick, how do I spell your last name?"

An Influencer type will say, "It certainly is a great day! How are you doing, David?" We respond with bonding, rapport, and empathy. Nearly 40 percent of the prospects and clients who call are Influencers. Please spend some time letting these people know you love them.

A Steady will speak softly and may even have a nervous chuckle or laugh. Please lower your voice. Allow for quiet and, more importantly, provide three options for them. For example, "We can get you in first thing in the morning, at noon, or around 4 pm." Do not rush the Steady.

A Compliant personality will respond like this: "This is David Tester calling regarding machine number 14752. There is a red wrench warning light blinking." With this client or prospect, stick to the facts, not the feelings.

Remember, no matter what they ask you for or what your service is, you should respond, "Absolutely." In a later chapter, I'll address what you should do in the event that you don't have the particular service they're requesting. But always ask for their first name, followed by, "Remind me how to spell your last name."

Your next line in the script is, "And just in case we get disconnected, your cell number is 208 . . ." Always lead with your local area code—in my state it's 208. Just remain silent and they will fill in the rest.

What do you do if their area code is not your local code? Great question. When they give you the phone number— let's say that it's (212) 123-4567—you follow up by asking, "Where is 212? Oh, New York. Upstate or the city?"

Now you have their name and phone number. You are still in charge of the phone call. However, the prospect *feels* like they are in charge of the call. You ask questions and they do the talking.

Here is the next line in the script: "Really quickly, how did you hear about us?"

This is critical for your marketing team. If they say, "Google," don't just say, "Okay." Ask where on Google. It could be on AdWords or it could be a review. Find out how people are hearing about you so you can do more marketing just like this.

The next line in our script is very simple: "Okay David, what has you calling us today?" Make sure to use their first name at least three times during the conversation.

Listen and take notes. Tell the prospect or customer, "I'm taking notes. Is that okay?" You don't have to ask for permission but when you do, you are subliminally telling the person, "I am listening to you."

Your job is not to educate the prospect—your only job is to book the appointment.

After the prospective client tells you why they are calling, add this line into the script: "Tell me more." And they *will* tell you more. Take notes and reiterate to the prospect or client what you are hearing from them. My motto is "Being listened to on the phone and being loved on the phone are so close together that most people cannot tell the difference." So listen and take notes and say things like "Tell me more."

If the reason for the call is some sort of problem, ask how long the problem has been an issue and what they have done to try to solve the problem. This is so you have a story to tell the salesperson or the doctor, but it also makes the prospect feel like they are being heard so they won't go somewhere else to solve their problem.

Next is the part where you earn your money. If you don't earn your money here, you throw it down the drain. The choice is yours.

"Would it make sense for me to invite you in? We can ask you some questions, you can ask us some questions, and after we are done, the two of us can determine the next step. I have an opening on Thursday morning or Friday at noon. What works best for you?"

We'll talk about booking the appointment properly in the next chapter. Right now, your mission is to sell the appointment and get an agreement. They may come in the door, make a Zoom call, or place a phone appointment in their day planner. That's your sole mission at this point.

Below is your script. Practice it on friends and family. The worst time to think of what to say is when it comes out of your mouth. Own this script.

"It's a great day at [your business name]! This is [your name]! How may I help you?"

The caller will respond in one of four ways, according to their personality type. The Dominant type will be bold and speak up, the Influencer will act interested and build rapport, the Steady style will slow down and embrace silence (when booking an appointment, offer three choices), and the Compliant type will stick to the facts, not feelings (never criticize them, and be detailed).

No matter what they ask for or want, respond with, "Absolutely. Really quickly, can I grab your first name, and remind me how to spell your last name."

"And, just in case we get disconnected, your cell number is 212 . . ." Lead with the area code closest to where your office is and write down the number they have.

What do you do if you find out you don't have the service or product they have asked for? Let's say the prospect asks if you work on diesel cars. Use the script "Discover and Does." Write that down.

After a brief hold, you say, "David, I have discovered we don't work on diesel cars. However, I found out who does. Do you have a pen?" Provide the prospect or client with three names and numbers.

After providing the names and numbers, ask the marketing question.

"How did you hear about us?"

They might say, "I heard about you in the newsletter!"

Ask just one follow-up question. "Oh, what did it say about us?"

Next, ask what caused them to call today, and remind the prospect that you are taking notes. "I'm taking notes. Is that okay?"

When they describe their problem, always say, "Tell me more." This allows you to discover why they are really calling.

Ask how long their problem has been an issue.

Ask what they have tried doing to solve the problem.

Repeat what you heard them say.

Next, invite them in for an appointment. "Would it make sense for me to invite you in? We can ask you some questions, you can ask us some questions, and then we can determine the next step."

Make sure you have two dates open and, if they are a Steady type, offer three dates. Let's pretend this prospect is a Steady.

"What works best for you? Monday morning, Wednesday at noon, or Friday afternoon?" With a Steady, please be quiet.

Always follow up with a reminder call, and if the prospect chooses not to come in, invite them back in again. Don't let them slip through a hole in your bucket of leads.

Over 80 percent of leads are not followed up on. Most front desk teams or customer service representatives are not trained to get these simple items:

- First name
- Last name
- Phone number
- How did you hear about us?
- Why are you calling?
- Tell me more
- How long has this been an issue?
- What have you done?
- Invitation for an appointment

Remember, a sixth grader can do this, so you and your team will be masters in no time at all! Take the script and practice. You only have to be 10 percent better than your competition to dominate your industry!

FEARLESS COMMUNICATION KEY TAKEAWAYS

- You must get their name and number and invite them in. Book the appointment.

- The worst time to think of what to say is when it comes out of your mouth. Practice your scripts!

- Listen and take notes.

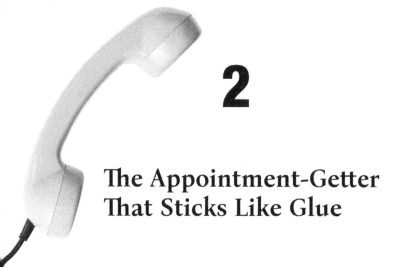

2

The Appointment-Getter That Sticks Like Glue

Many prospects say yes to an appointment just to get off the phone. By following my system, cancellation or no-show rates can be reduced by as much as 65 percent. An appointment must be in the prospect or client's day planner.

Too often, we think a prospect saying okay or sending a Google invite is an unequivocal yes to the consultation or appointment. One of the biggest time wasters and causes of lost revenue is no-shows on appointments. Think of the time involved to generate each lead, create an appointment, and prepare the sales consultant or coordinator for the meeting—all of that preparation and investment only to have the prospect fail to show.

It's worth your time to do the math. In the automotive repair industry, a lost lead or prospect that you don't record a name and number for can cost $381 per call. The average repair is $550, and in one year that client can be worth $4,500 in lost revenue.

On average, if you lose three to five leads per day by not following our system, just the cost of generating those leads is a loss of nearly $2,000 per day. If you could convert 30 percent of those leads in a week (seven out of 25 leads), you would have generated a *new* $3,850. If the average yearly value of a client is $4,500, that number jumps to $31,500 with just one new client a week.

It's a big enough number that you cannot afford to *not* invest in training your front desk staff. They must be trained to answer the phone correctly and to book the consultation using the appointment-getter that sticks like glue. Perhaps a better question for you to answer is "Can I afford to let that much money leave my business through the phone line each week?"

A business owner I started coaching said to me, "Dave, that's a lot of money. But what if I implement your system, train my employee to be a first-class Director of First Impressions, and they leave me in six months to go work somewhere else?"

I told the client, "This is an excellent perspective. I don't blame you one bit for thinking that. However, do you know what's worse than training your Director of First Impressions and having them leave? *Not* training them and having them stay with you."

The concept behind the appointment-getter is to put a wall around the prospect that they cannot get around—don't allow them to slip out of the lead bucket. Remember, after they call your office, they are going to talk to friends, family members, and even your competition about the solution they are looking for. Make sure you appear to be booked so solid that if they did miss the appointment, they would never have a shot at a second chance.

I once asked my wife, Claudia, "How come you never miss a hair appointment?"

She said, "I waited a year to get in to see these people, and if I miss my slot, they will give it away and I'll never get back in again."

Make sure you build enough value in selling the appointment to your prospect that you find yourself not only working by referral only but also by appointment only.

Part 1: "So, [client name], based on what we have talked about today, would it make sense for me to invite you in for a consultation? We can ask you some questions, you can ask us some questions, and we can determine what the next step will be."

The great part of asking the prospect if you can invite them in is this: We *invite* friends and family into our home. Always ask if it would make sense to *invite* them in.

Part 2: Ensure there's an opening in your day planner. You need to lead the way in proposing a date. I like to propose three dates—never more than three, but never less than two.

"Scott, I have an opening on Tuesday at 3 p.m., Wednesday first thing in the morning, or Friday at noon. What works best for you?"

I will touch on personality types later on in the book, but by using the DISC personality assessment, I know that some personality types need three options and time to think it over. This allows the prospect to feel like they are in charge by selecting the correct date. However, you should lead the way and not say things like "What works best for you?" Don't be so flexible that you sound like a sales company. It should appear that you are booked solid and there's simply no room for cancellations or no-shows.

Part 3: We have now established a day and time for the appointment. In this case it's going to be Tuesday at 3 p.m. This move is not magic or ground-breaking—I get it. However, if you can get your team to just embrace this one tactic, no-show numbers will decline immediately.

Use the magic phrase, "Shall I put that in pen or in pencil?"

The prospect can respond in a number of ways. My favorite response is "Go ahead and put it in pen." Pen sticks, but pencil can be erased or canceled. The prospect can also respond by saying, "Let's put it in pencil." Do not write an appointment in pencil. If you don't value your process or your coordinator's time enough to book it in pen, don't waste time even inviting people into your office.

The response is very simple. "Let's find a time when you can book that in pen. We certainly don't want to waste our time, but more than anything we don't want to waste *your* time. Would Friday at noon work better?" Again, this might feel awkward for your customer service representative at first. But once cancellations stop, they will feel more comfortable following a script that works.

You may get a response that sounds something like this: "Say what? Pen or pencil?"

You can quickly respond, "Pen sticks, but pencil can be erased. Is this a time that will stick in pen for you?"

Part 4: This is a process that requires more than one step. The idea is to eliminate cancellations and keep prospects from using appointments as a way to delay action or, even worse, to get off the phone.

The next part of your script reads, "You don't see anything between now and [the appointment date] that will keep you from making the appointment?"

Let's pause here for a reminder. If there is a holiday before or after, or if it's on a Friday afternoon, please don't pretend it's not going to happen. Remind the prospect if it's the Friday before Labor Day or the Thursday before Memorial Day weekend. This is a very subtle move, but it's better to address it now than get a phone call the day before saying, "Oh, I forgot. This is a long weekend. I can't show up."

Part 5: The last part of the script is the most difficult. However, this is the part that seals the deal. If you aren't recording your calls on both ends, please start now. My philosophy is what gets measured gets done. If you aren't recording your calls and coaching your team, they will always give you a distorted version of the call. I've found that there's the customer service representative's (CSR) version of the call, and then there's what *actually* took place on the call.

"My biggest fear is that we will book the appointment for next week, the doctor will prepare for your consultation, and you will call in right before the appointment and cancel. Is it just me or is that often the case?"

Nine times out of ten, people will say, "That's just you."

I respond, "We will see you next Tuesday at 3 p.m."

Note my key words in the script: "my *biggest* fear." I'm not projecting on them. Rather, I'm saying that this is *my* biggest fear.

Last, I state, "Is that just me, or is that the case?" By saying this, I'm trying to make the prospect feel okay. If I make a statement like "You won't show up, right?"

I make the prospect/customer feel defensive. If I state "my fear is" it places the burden on me, and it keeps me from projecting.

Similarly, instead of saying, "Are you mad at me?" I might say, "I get the feeling that I have offended you. Is that the case or is it just me?" I always want to make the person on the other end of the telephone feel okay. Remember, sometimes an appointment can be a form of a put-off or an objection. Some people book an appointment just to get us off the phone. We make it okay for them to tell us, "I probably won't show up" or "Yes, I will show up on time, and you can put that in ink."

Take your time to practice this script and own it.

After the call, I send the client a Google invite. I also send a handwritten card in the mail thanking them for their time, saying something like "We look forward to seeing you on Tuesday at 3 p.m."

Finally, I always make a reminder call the day before.

You need an appointment-getter that sticks like glue. If you use this program, there's a good chance you could either save or make your company a quarter of a million dollars in lost leads every year.

FEARLESS COMMUNICATION KEY TAKEAWAYS

- Lost leads equal lost revenue. How many leads are you losing every day because the phone is not being answered correctly?

- An appointment is a form of an objection. Book it in ink.

- Don't educate. Sell the value of the appointment.

3

The Director of
First Impressions

This is my favorite chapter in this book.

When we do live calls with the tool I'm going to cover in this chapter, people are always amazed because they find out one of two things: their customers are either big fans, or things are not going as well as they had thought.

Before I begin the script for the Director of First Impressions, I'd like to remind you of the "why" behind the "what."

Why do we make these phone calls? The majority of your clients are already on your competitors' hit lists. In other words, your competitors are prospecting your clients. They're likely telling your customers things like this:

"We return phone calls, and *they* do not."

"We follow up, and *they* do not."

"We are in your office right now. When was the last time *they* visited you in person?"

"We listen, and *they* do not."

"We fix issues, but *they* do not."

"If we do make a mistake, *our* company is fast and consistent in correcting it."

You might ask, "Dave, they wouldn't say stuff like that about us, would they?"

Yes, they would. And yes, they do. Keep in mind that 20 percent of your current customer base is thinking about leaving you. They believe you don't care and that you take their business for granted. Depending on how you use my book, this might be the most important chapter you read (and hopefully implement). When I ask you, "When is the most important time to tell your significant other you love them?" the answer must always be "Before someone else does."

Let's build a plan to call your customers and tell them how much you love them today. I would encourage you to have a plan for 30-day, 60-day, 90-day, six-month, and one-year-old clients. Your calls should rotate all the time so no client ever gets overlooked.

For sales teams, I coach this concept as "Three by Nine." Simply call three current customers every morning before 9 a.m., using the script we'll cover in this chapter. The goal of this call is to thank your customers.

When you are coaching your team, it's very easy to sell them on this concept. They may ask, "Why do we have to call?"

Remind the team that the call has multiple goals:

1. Make your customers feel appreciated.

2. Provide a system for staying in touch with customers.

3. Create a wall around your customer base that the competitors can't get around by protecting and serving your customers.

4. Discover what you can do better. (This is also a great time to share a new product or cross-sell!)

5. Ask for a referral and a recommendation. (Most of your customers want to help you, but you just don't ask them enough.)

6. Listen for what's *not* being said. (If you hear words like "good," "okay," and "fine," you have a customer service emergency!)

The standard script always starts by interrupting the customer's expectations. Some people ask me why we don't identify our company right away. Let's be honest—you are still considered a salesperson. We need to disrupt the typical customer's expectations of a salesperson.

Start by sharing who you are so they don't have an excuse to say, "We'll call you back," or "I'll take a message." Those are just code words for "Go away."

(The customer is A & D Dentist, and I'm the salesperson)

Ring. Ring.

"Hello, this is A & D Dentist. How may I help you?"

"Hey, it's me, Dave. Did I catch you at a bad time?"

"No. Dave who?"

"Dave Tester, I'm the Director of First Impressions for a company called Jon Carson Consulting. Does that ring a bell?"

Let's leave the script for a minute. If the name of your company does *not* ring a bell with the customer, you have an issue. The salesperson or owner needs to jump in the car immediately and pay a visit to the customer. In this case, it will ring a bell.

"Oh yes, Dave. We love your live training and coaching. We feel so much more confident on the phone since you started training us. Thank you."

"We get that a lot. What do you like best from our training?"

"I think I would have to say managing the different personalities and when you make the live phone calls in front of us during training."

Let's step out of the script again. This is why I dig deep here—I want to get real "Testermonials." I can either record these with permission or I can transcribe them. Remember, if *you* tell prospects how great you are, it's considered a sales technique. However, if your customers say it, it's considered the truth. Slow down during this part of the call. When you're training your team, instruct your team members to remain silent when the customer is talking. They need to just listen to the customer's feedback.

Now, back to the script.

"When you say, 'managing the personalities,' please tell me more."

"Sure. You've helped me zero in on the dominant characteristics of the DISC profile. I used to think the Dominant types were mad at me, but now I know they just tend to talk loudly. So I speak up to match them. It gives me more confidence."

"Thank you very much. Is it okay if we use what you have said today for marketing and referrals?"

"Of course."

"Also, we are always working on improving—is there anything we can do better to serve you?"

You must listen for what's not being said here. If they don't remember you or don't have a lot of good things to say, you have to spend some time at this part of the script to find out what the issue is. My motto is "Bad news is not like wine—it doesn't get better with time." You have to find out what is wrong because nothing can change until the unspoken is said and heard.

"I think you do a really good job. Sometimes you may try to cram too much into our session. It's a lot of information and sometimes you might move a little too fast through it."

"Okay. Great. I want to make sure you know that I'm taking notes. Is that okay?" (I tell the customer this so they know I'm listening.)

"Absolutely."

"Thank you. What would you like to see happen in those training sessions?"

"Let me think." (Please be quiet here.) "If you could leave us a copy of your slide deck, or better yet a recording, we could go over the training again after you've left. That would be very helpful."

"Okay, I'm writing this down. Leave a copy of the PowerPoint behind and possibly a recording. Did I miss anything else?"

"No, I think that's it. Overall, we really love the training."

"Perfect. Real quick, is there one thing that you would say is particularly outstanding in my training or something you might tell someone else about if they asked you to recommend Dave Tester?"

"I would tell them the live phone calls are the game changer. Sometimes trainers or speakers just tell us to do things. You coach and encourage us, but then you ask for the phone number and call the customer right in front of us. You model the techniques that you teach, live and in-person, and it works! That's what is memorable and what I tell others about."

"Wow. Thank you so much. Before I let you go, I was going to ask who do you know that we should know? Is there anyone in your circle who could use coaching on the phone to help customer care or improve sales?"

Keep in mind that usually they don't know anybody, but they will say, "Let me think about it and I will get back with you."

One more time, let's step out of the script. This is a perfect time to set up an account review or a drop-in for a customer-care person or salesperson from your office. The final part of the script reads like this:

> "Remember the number one reason I am calling you is to tell you thank you for your business. Our motto here at Jon Carson Consulting is 'If you like what we do, tell others. If we can ever do anything better, please tell me.'"

End the call and transcribe the notes or pull the recording. Please drop a handwritten thank-you note in the mail and follow up again, depending on where this first call falls: the 30-day, 60-day, 90-day, six-month, or one-year plan. Schedule the next call today.

Remember, clients don't care what you say. They care how you make them feel. Make your customers feel great with the Director of First Impressions script.

FEARLESS COMMUNICATION KEY TAKEAWAYS

- The majority of your clients are already on your competitors' hit lists, so build a wall around them by making follow up calls.

- Build a plan to call your customers and tell them how much you love them today.

- Clients don't care what you say—they care how you make them feel.

4

How to Get a Five-Star Google Review

This chapter has two elements: The first is finding out how a customer heard about your business, and the second is asking for a five-star Google review.

We'll start with how they heard about you. This element of the call uses a review of the script in chapter 1, "How Did You Hear About Us?" Asking this question supports the marketing team and allows you to observe what the customer is seeking.

When the answer is Google, it's absolutely imperative to ask *what* they heard about you on Google. There are two types of shoppers on Google. One type is strictly looking for the cheapest price. The other type is looking for reviews and ratings.

If they tell you, 'We found you at the top of the list,' you have a great search engine optimization team. However, beware—the number one concern for this type of prospect is still price.

Remember to always ask a question in response to a question. For example, a customer at a tire shop might ask, "How much is it for a set of four tires?" Your reply should be something like "That's a great question! Are you asking for a reason?"

Since you know they found you at the top of the Google search results, you know price is important. In some cases, it will be the *most* important thing to the customer. If so, the customer's answer will likely be "I'm looking around for quotes on tires. I'm trying to find a good price." You may get an even simpler answer such as "I want to know how much the price is for a set of tires."

Don't forget that you're still on script before you quote the customer a price. Your next question should be "Is price your only concern?" Thirty-five percent of our shoppers at the time of this writing care *only* about price. If they tell you price is indeed their top concern, give them the cheapest price on the lowest model that you can find. However, 65 percent of your prospects at the time of this writing are looking for *value*. The reason I give you the Google script is so you don't mistakenly try to sell price to a value customer or vice versa.

This brings us to the second part of the chapter, which is key to building a wall around your customer base and giving your prospects a real reason to choose you instead of any of their other options—it's another patch for your leaky bucket. Asking for a five-star Google review will make all of the difference.

Most Directors of First Impressions don't ask for a Google review. The reason for this is very simple: They don't like to be asked for Google reviews themselves. We sell the same way we buy, and we give customer service the way we like to receive it.

Please stop doing this. In our training, we require you to ask for a five-star Google review. The good news is it will be much easier because you no longer have to wing it when asking! You have a script to follow. I will remind you time and time again of the importance of following your script. The worst time to think of something to say is when it comes out of your mouth.

This concept is closely tied to the last chapter, so please master chapter 3 before asking for a five-star Google review.

In this example, the customer is pleased with the service you provide. Always ask, "What did you like best about working with our company?" You can also ask, "What was most memorable about working with our company?"

If only restaurant managers at high-end eating establishments asked the same questions! Instead, they come out and ask something bland like "How was everything?" That question is way too easy to answer with a "fine" or an "okay." If they asked what you liked best or what the most memorable part of your meal was, I guarantee it would lead to more five-star reviews. Furthermore, if anything was not perfect, they could solve the issue on the spot.

After your new client tells you what they like best, always ask, "Could we have done anything better?" Later in the book, I will provide you with a script for bad experiences or upset customers. For now, we'll treat the situation as if the customer is satisfied completely. Next, ask the client, "If you were to recommend us to others, what would you tell them about us?" Again, if you master chapter 3, the script leads perfectly into getting a five-star review.

When they tell you what they would tell others, it's important to record the conversation or take notes. In your tone of voice, assume they are ready to give you a five-star review.

Your next statement should be "Would you be willing to recommend us to others?" I always use the customer's name in this statement: "Tom, it sounds like you would be willing to recommend Tester Broadcast to others." After they say yes, I have already laid the groundwork for the next step.

"Tom, would you be willing to give us a five-star Google review?"

The customer can choose to go a couple of different directions at this point. The *best* option is a simple, "Yes, I will." However, it's not always quite that easy. The second option for the customer usually goes something like this: "I don't know how to do that," or "My computer is too cumbersome to do that." They could cut straight to the point and just say, "I don't give reviews." Ouch.

For ease of illustration, let's stick to the "yes" or "My computer is too hard to navigate." In these cases, ask for the customer's email address very quickly. Some people would say that this should be done early on the call, but I've discovered that it's much wiser to hold off on asking for it upfront because *we* don't like when people ask for our email addresses. But we do expect you to ask for five-star reviews and get the email address where you can send the link.

Here is the script for asking for the email:

"Can you remind me of your email, Tom? It's tom@gmail.com?" I use their first name with gmail.com. I do this for two reasons: First, I would like a Gmail account because it is tied into Google and makes giving a five-star review easier. Second, of course their email is not tom@gmail.com—I'm well aware of that. However, they will correct me with their *actual* email address. They'll willingly share it once I have started the conversation with my lead-in. I suggest you have one of two links to send out. One link should be a Google link if the customer has Gmail, and the other should be a home web page review.

You also have a couple of other options for encouraging Google reviews. You can challenge your staff with a gift card incentive each month. The member of your team who collects the most reviews is rewarded with a gift card or another incentive. Conversely, you can reward your client for providing you with a five-star review by giving *them* the gift card.

Google reviews and "Testermonials" are vitally important to your continuing growth as a business and to keep your lead bucket strong. Please follow my script and ask for both. If you tell customers and prospects how good you are, it's considered a sales tactic. However, if your customers say it themselves, it's considered the truth. Use the checklist below to help you achieve success in this essential part of your business.

- When a customer calls to tell you how great you are or when you call to check in, remember to *listen.* Don't talk.
- When they say, "Mark was great," say, "Tell me more."
- "When you say outstanding communication, please tell me more."
- "If you were to recommend our company to someone, what would you tell them about us or about your experience?"
- "It sounds like you would be willing to recommend us. Would it be okay to ask you for a five-star Google review?"
- "What did you like best about working with our company? What was most memorable about working with our company?"
- "Could we have done anything better?"
- "Remind me of your email. It's chris@gmail.com?"
- Send out a prepared Google review link so all they have to do is click on it.

Five-star Google reviews win.

FEARLESS COMMUNICATION KEY TAKEAWAYS

- There are two types of shoppers on Google: those who are looking for the cheapest price, and those who are looking for reviews and ratings. Find out what's important to your prospect by asking, "What did you see on Google?"

- Always ask a question in response to a question. "That's a great question! Are you asking for a reason?"

- Remember to ask for a five-star Google review. If you don't ask for a five star, you will not get a five star.

5

The Volcano Theory and the Upset Customer

When the phone rings, these are our two biggest fears:

1. What if they're mad at me?
2. What if they ask a question that I don't know the answer to?

The Volcano Theory is about turning an upset customer into a raving fan. It deals with the biggest fear of anyone answering the phone at a business, including myself.

You remember the drill, right? A dog was dropped off and the client was mad because Dr. Tester wasn't on hand. I thought I was in trouble with my dad and assumed the customer was upset at me for not making their wishes happen. It turns out that that wasn't the case at all. My dad was upset at the client for dressing me down and the client was just worried about his dog.

The reason I call this the Volcano Theory is that some folks erupt like a volcano when they're mad. However, it's essential to remember that a volcanic eruption eventually starts to cool off.

It's important to note the customer is not mad at *you*. The customer is upset about the situation. Please focus on the problem, not the person. Do not take the call personally, no matter how loud they are. You may think, "Easy for you to say, Dave."

At no time should you ever take abuse on the phone. If it gets too hot, simply ask the customer, "Are you mad at me?" or "I get the feeling you're mad at me. Is that the case?" Use this as a trigger to lower the temperature of the client or, in some cases, to remind them to tone it down.

If at any time they tell you that they're upset at you (assuming that you're just the messenger of the bad news), please take their name and number and let them know the owner or your supervisor will be calling them back. This has not happened to any of my students, but it has happened during a coaching session and we defused it immediately.

The bottom line is that you should not be fearful of upset customers. The upcoming script will help you master that skill. However, if at any time the customer is mad at you, please pass the call on to a supervisor or owner.

In Sun Tzu's book *The Art of War*, one of the key concepts is to fight the battle before it even starts. Work out the plan and all of the potential scenarios ahead of time. As a result, before the battle even begins, you will have won the war. Keep in mind, however, that the goal is not to win. Your goal is this:

1. Make sure that the customer feels they are being heard.

2. Identify the next step to clean up the situation.

3. Set a date for a follow up.

If done correctly, you will have created a fan of your company for life. Customers remember and talk about how we deal with missteps far more often than they do with outstanding service. The key is to turn a potential customer service failure into a genuine opportunity to shine.

Let's begin with the process.

When you sense a customer is upset or you are calling an upset customer back, open with, "I get the feeling that we did something wrong. Please tell me what happened."

The most important part of this script is to not say a word. Let them vent. Remember, this is the volcano—the louder or hotter they get, the softer you should get.

When it is appropriate or when you feel like they have finished their vent session, continue with the next step.

"I don't know how you feel, but I do understand. I'm taking notes. Is that okay?"

In trainings, I sometimes receive pushback on this line. Front desk teams will ask me, "How do you understand but you don't know how they feel?"

I have no way of knowing how you feel or where you are coming from because I'm not walking in your shoes or living in your head. But I *can* understand because I am taking notes. I write down what the customer says so I can comprehend what led them to *feel* that way. Just to make sure the customer knows I am listening, I add, "I'm taking notes. Is that okay?"

Most people don't truly listen to complaints. They may blame management or corporate, but they almost certainly feel that they cannot do anything to solve the problem. This script empowers you to ensure that the customer is heard, find out what happened and what should have happened, and discover what will happen next.

Never, and I mean *never*, tell the customer you are sorry. Everyone in the country is sorry. No one really cares. People all around us are saying, "I'm sorry," and yet do nothing.

You do not need to say you are sorry. Instead, say, "That's not like us. We always try our best, but we don't always succeed in delivering our best." This tells the client that you are listening. Have their first and last name ready so you can follow up. "Mr. Tester, tell me what *should* have happened."

This gives the customer a chance to vent again, only this time without all of the emotion. It is a very simple discussion of what should have happened and provides a chance for them to tell you more about the issue. It's your golden opportunity to find out what the *real* problem is—the problem with the problem. Sometimes I like to refer to it as "the question behind the question."

When in doubt, say to the customer, "You said it was leaking when you returned to your home; *tell me more*."

"Tell me more" is the magic phrase. Continue to follow the script. The real secret of the Volcano Theory is that you are always in control of the situation. The customer is doing all of the talking, but you are asking all of the questions.

"Tell me, Mr. Tester, what would you like to see happen now?"

When we first go over the script, many people think that the customer is going to ask for a monster truck and a winning lottery ticket. I provided customer-care training for 44 Carl's Junior and Hardees restaurants. Over a two-month period, I called customers back who complained. They were stunned that a fast food chain would call back on a complaint. Nine times out of ten, they didn't want a gift card or anything free. They just wanted hot chicken or a cooked hamburger.

When we ask, "What would you like to see happen next?" nine times out of ten, all the customer wants is to resolve the issue. That's it. Please note that I'm not empowering you to tell the customer, "Yes, we will do it." Rather, I'm empowering you to find out what the customer would like to see happen next.

The following question on the script reads like this: "If we can do that, then what will happen?" Never assume that if you fix the problem, the customer will give you a five-star review or stay off Facebook. They may bash you no matter what, so always ask, "If we do that, then what will happen?"

You now have a clear next step. Read your written notes back to the customer. It sounds like this: "Just to make sure we are on the same page, Dave, I'm hearing you say that, A, B, and C are broken. Did I hear you correctly?" They may add to or clarify what you just played back.

Now break down what will happen next.

"Within the next 10 days, one of my team members will call you back on this number. I'm not promising you whether they will fix it or not. However, they will have a clear next step for A, B, and C. Is that okay, Mr. Tester?"

After they respond, reinforce your goals:

1. Make sure the customer feels like they are being heard.

2. Provide clear next steps on cleaning up the situation.

3. Set a date for a follow up call.

If done correctly, you have created a fan of your company for life.

"Dave, I want you to know that you are being heard and that you are important to us." Wait for some sort of a response. "Is it okay if I pass on these notes to our team so you can get a clear next step in the next 10 days?"

After they respond, let them know that if for some reason they don't get a follow-up call, they may call you directly and *you* will make sure they get a call.

At the end of the call, I add, "Our motto is, 'If you like what we do, tell others.' However, if we can ever do anything better, like solving A, B and C, please tell me, okay? Thank you again for your call."

Your goal is to win the battle before it even starts. A benefit of this approach is that you will no longer panic when the phone rings. The customer might be mad, but they are not mad at you. So focus on the problem, not the person.

- When a customer is angry, let them explode. Be quiet, because the louder you get the louder they will get.

- If the customer gets too loud, simply ask, "Are you mad at me?" or "I get the feeling you're mad at me. Is that the case?" Use this to remind them to tone it down.

- When you sense a customer is upset or you are calling an upset customer back, open with, "I get the feeling that we did something wrong. Please tell me what happened."

- "I don't know how you feel, but I understand. I'm taking notes. Is that okay?"

- "When you say broken, please tell me more."

- "Let me play back what I'm hearing you say. Is that correct?" Take notes and read them back to the customer and ask if you got everything correct. Then explain to them how your team will follow up to solve the problem.

- "That's not like us. We try our best, but we don't always do our best. Mr. Tester, what should have happened?"

- "What would you like to see happen now? If I can do that, what will happen?"

- Get a clear next step.

FEARLESS COMMUNICATION KEY TAKEAWAYS

- An upset customer is not mad at *you*. They're upset about the situation. Focus on the problem, not the person.

- Customers remember how you deal with missteps far more than outstanding service. Turn a potential customer service failure into a five-star Google review.

- Most people don't truly listen to complaints. Empathy and follow-up win the day!

6

Listen for DISC

Wouldn't it be nice if each client or prospect who called began the conversation by telling us how they would like to be treated? I'm not just talking about prospects wanting superior customer service. It would be nice if they would say something like this:

- "Speak loudly."
- "Give me three choices."
- "I like to think things over."
- "Can we just spend some time bonding and talking?"

If only that were the case, right? Just imagine how much easier that would make our jobs! Here's the good news: this isn't just some sales fantasy. We have discovered the secret to determining how people want to be treated on the phone. In fact, the secret is not really a secret at all. It begins with our greeting.

"It's a great day at Tester Broadcasting! This is Dave. How may I help you?"

I've trained this opening line long enough that I've heard many of my listeners say things like "It's not genuine," or, "I don't like to say it. It doesn't sound right."

As with all of our scripts and techniques, there is a reason behind the wording. You may not be having a great day, and the prospect may not either, but this opening line puts you in a position of *control*.

Remember, the ultimate job of answering the phone is to control the call. When you use this opening line, the client or prospect will respond in one of several ways, which will give you a solid clue about how they want to be treated on the phone.

If the person on the other end of the line is an Influencer personality, here is how they respond to the greeting: "Well, it certainly is a great day! How are you?" It could also be some version of, "You sure sound friendly on the phone!" "I love your attitude," or "Sorry to bother you with this question, but . . ."

When you hear this kind of response, you should go into your Influencer script mode. You don't have to *be* an Influencer, but you must stretch to *reach* an Influencer personality. Keep in mind, you have to *act* or at least try to be interested in what the caller is saying. (Please slow down at this point in the call and take notes.) Use words like "love" ("I love that about you") and "family" ("We are all in this together as a family"), or the best statement is "Tell me more." Know that the prospect or client will tell you more, so slow down and listen.

The key to working with this prospect or client is making them *feel* loved on the phone. You don't have to tell them you love them, but you may want to say, "I love that you love us." You'll connect with an Influencer in about four out of every 10 dials.

When booking an appointment, an Influencer may mislead you just a bit so you will still love them. They may say, "I will book the appointment, but I have to check with my wife first." They could also tell you something like "I'm pretty sure we are going to come down to your office, but I just need to check on a couple of things first." Stick to your script and use the Appointment-Getter That Sticks Like Glue from earlier in the book. You can also tell them, "It's okay to say no. Even if you tell me that you're not coming, we will still be friends." An Influencer personality's number one fear is not being loved. Please make this personality type feel loved.

The Compliant personality is a conscientious individual who responds to your greeting with facts only.

"It's a great day at My Copier and Printer Company! This is Dave. How may I help you?"

The Compliant customer will generally lead with facts. "I am calling about Xerox model number 1427452A. The red wrench is showing on the screen and, based on my data, it is time for a memory update."

This personality type is almost the opposite of the Influencer. Where the Influencer wants feelings, the Compliant wants just the facts. Their biggest fear is being wrong or incorrect.

Repeat the digits of the model number back to them, or whatever information they open with. Steer away from small talk with this group and stick to your script. Your response in this case should be "Absolutely. I heard you say Xerox model number 14 27 45 2 A. Remind me of your first name." From here, transition into your script.

Stick exclusively to facts. You should also amend the script to sound like this: "Just to make sure we are on the same page, let me play back what I'm hearing you say. The red wrench is showing on the screen and, based on your data, you're pretty sure it's time for a memory update. Did I miss anything?" Focus on getting the details absolutely correct. The Compliant customer would also like to move the process along as quickly as possible. This personality makes up about two out of 10 of your incoming calls.

The Dominant personality is a decisive individual, and they make up less than two out of 10 calls. This is typically the second-most easily identifiable personality on the phone.

To discover a person's personality type, you are listening for what is *not* being said on your phone calls. For example, the Dominant personality might be on speaker phone and you'll hear others in the background. They may even talk to someone else in their office while calling and go so far as to ask you to hold for a minute. In some cases, this might strike you as rude. It's just a personality trait, though, so don't sweat it.

With the Dominant, you'll again want to focus on feelings rather than facts. "It's a great day at Dialing Strangers! This is Dave. How may I help you?"

Their response usually begins with a first name. They may sound like they assume you should know every issue they have ever had with your company or product. "This is Tom, and I can't get my sales team to make phone calls. Your damn book doesn't work."

I know you'll struggle to believe me, but in spite of how it seems, this person is *not* mad at you. One of the greatest fears of customer service representatives is "What if they're mad at me?" Speak up and be bold. Twenty seconds of insane courage will change your life.

"Tom, that's not like us. I want you to win with your sales team. Real quick, remind me how to spell your last name."

Please notice the key word—I want Tom to *win*. The Dominant personality has two fears: being taken advantage of and not winning. Lead into your script by assuring them they are going to *win*.

Follow up with, "Tom, we want to make sure no one takes advantage of you. Real quick, remind me of your cell phone number?" If Tom is a current customer, you can also say, "Tom, remind me where you are calling from." Again, stick to the script, but speak up. That does not mean speak faster, but always be strong and bold. You don't have to be dominant. Just pretend like you are a dominant personality.

Let me remind you one more time that even though they are loud on the phone, the Dominant is *not* mad at you. They just happen to speak loudly. Match the tone and tempo. Speak with confidence.

The Steady personality may be the most difficult for you to pick up on. They tend to hang out somewhere between Influencer and Compliant. What I have discovered is that a Steady will lead with first and last name after the intentional "great day" greeting.

"This is Dave Tester, and I'm calling from Fearless Communication. We are looking for help on printing." The tone will be much softer, and you may even hear a nervous chuckle. Please don't mirror that chuckle or nervous laugh. Be quiet, speak softly, and follow the script. One of the keys to effectively connecting with the Steady is to never rush them into a decision.

This example might be helpful. You might naturally tend to ask, "Would you like us to come out this morning or in the afternoon?" To reach the Steady, however, amend that to "What would work best for you? Would you like us to come out this morning, around the lunch hour, or later on this after-noon?" Please do not say anything else. This person needs time to think, because they want to provide you with the correct answer. Sometimes this is the most challenging personality to pick up on, but if you are listening with intent to understand the client (and not just listening with intent to respond), you can become very adept at this skill.

Within the first seven seconds of a phone call, you should start picking up clues to the personality type you're speaking with. Unfortunately, the person on the other end will not come out and say, "I'm an Influencer, love on me!" This means you have to get so good at this skill that people simply cannot ignore you.

It's a great day at my business, because I follow a script and I know the next words out of the prospect's mouth will give me a clue about how they want to be communicated with. Practice makes perfect. Practice this skill first, and then implement it. Listening with intent will change your phone skill from average to one of the best in the business.

This is what will *truly* make it a great day at your office.

- The Influencer type opens with, "It certainly is a great day! How are you?" or "Sorry to bother you with a question." They may laugh. They want to feel loved and are concerned with making others happy. Act interested in what they're saying.

- The Compliant personality focuses on the facts. Their biggest fear is being incorrect. They may be short and to the point. When talking to a Compliant type, omit small talk and stick with facts. They usually want to get through the call as quickly as possible.

- The Dominant type is decisive and wants to win. Listen for what is *not* being said to identify this personality type—they're often distracted or may have background noise. They may lead with their name, and they often speak loudly. Focus on feelings rather than facts. Speak up and be bold. The Dominant personality has two fears: being taken advantage of and not winning. Lead into your script by assuring them they are going to *win*.

- The Steady personality is somewhere between the Influencer and Compliant and will often open with their first and last name. They tend to have a softer tone. Speak softly and never rush them into a decision. Always give a Steady three options and let them have time to think.

FEARLESS COMMUNICATION KEY TAKEAWAYS

- The ultimate job of answering the phone is to follow the script and control the call.

- To discover a person's personality type, listen to the tone and tempo of the caller. Listen, don't talk.

- Listening with intent will change your phone skill from average to one of the best in the business. Be so good at what you do people cannot ignore you.

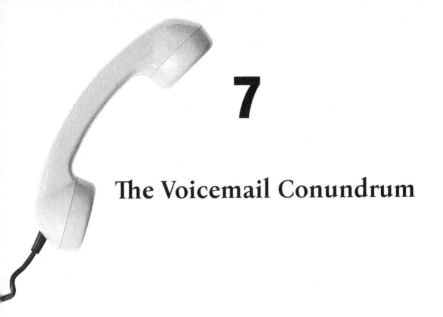

7

The Voicemail Conundrum

"I left a voicemail, but I haven't heard back."

Those can be the most frustrating words for an owner of a company to hear from the Director of First Impressions about following up with a client or prospect. Think about it. Why do we typically call a client? Often it's to get an approval on a work order, process, or procedure, or to provide an update or status report. These are significant pieces of the puzzle that will ultimately build a successful business.

While the Director of First Impressions waits on a return voicemail, the entire staff has to sit and wait as well. For growing companies, time is money. And while money may be refundable, time most certainly is not. Luckily, we've discovered four ways to get your voicemail message returned.

Before we start the process, you must agree that the goal of leaving a voicemail is to get a return call. Too many people who make phone calls hope that they reach voicemail so they don't have to talk to a live person. I sincerely hope this doesn't describe you—you're letting customers leak out of your bucket if that's the case. If you don't want the client, prospect, or customer to call you back, please do not use our system. But if the goal of the voicemail is to get a return call, continue reading this chapter.

Most people don't spend much time listening to the customer's voicemail greeting. If you reach voicemail when making a call, you are typically thinking about other things or just waiting for the beep rather than planning what you should say.

This is a scripted system. Own your script. The worst time to think of what to say is when it comes out of your mouth. First, slow down your mind and listen to the person's voicemail greeting on the other end. That is the secret to getting a return phone call. You will match the script with the type of greeting they leave on their voicemail message.

This process is an art form. It is not a science. The voicemail personality type is based on the thousands of phone calls I have made, recorded, and documented over the years. It may not always work to perfection, but for the most part, these four tips work like magic to get customers to return your call.

The number one challenge is to avoid leaving a long voicemail. Unfortunately, the typical message people leave on a client's voicemail averages between 55 seconds and one minute and 30 seconds. Some messages would no doubt go even longer, but thank heavens, the recording usually stops at about two minutes.

My first secret is this: less is more. In fact, in some cases, if you say nothing and just hang up, 20 percent of the people you call will actually call back because they are just curious to see who called them. Less is more.

The number two challenge that we face is using the word "love" in our voicemail messages. "I would *love* to hear from you." "I would *love* to get together." "I would *love* for you to call me back." Please, do us all a favor and stop using "love" all the time in your voicemail messages! I will teach you where love fits in. However, 51 percent of voicemail messages have "love" in them. Customers start tuning out this sort of redundancy, so stop using "love" until we tell you it's okay.

THE DOMINANT TYPE

Remember, the key is to *listen* to the client, customer, or prospect's voicemail greeting. What do they have on their recording? Here is what I want you to listen for.

1. The Dominant's greeting is very short.

2. It usually doesn't include "have a good day" or "goodbye." It's just short.

3. The message may sound like it was recorded in a vehicle or on speaker phone.

Here's an example: "This is Dave. I'm not in. You know what to do." Then the phone beeps. If the average voicemail message is over one minute long, you need to shorten the Dominant's message to less than 10 seconds. And you should *not* say goodbye.

Here is your script for the Dominant voicemail message. After the tone, be bold (not fast) and speak up.

"Hey, it's me, (your name). I think it might be important that you call me back. (Your phone number)." At this point, disconnect the call.

The key phrase here is "I think it might be important." Do *not* change this script line. If you believe in yourself, your product, or your company, this voicemail message works almost every time.

On occasion, I've been known to take this concept even one step further. I sometimes leave no phone number at all. That's right—I will simply say, "Hey, it's me, Dave. I think it's important that you call me back." Without hesitation, I disconnect the line. Remember, the Dominant personality wants nothing more than to *win*. They fear being taken advantage of. They *want* to return that phone call.

My million-dollar tip? Hang up the phone when you hear the customer call you back. Then, immediately call them right back. The customer will more than likely pick up. You now control the call, so be prepared and don't hang up when they say hello.

THE INFLUENCER TYPE

Here is where we let in the love—the Influencer personality voicemail. This will be about four out of 10 of your phone calls, while the Dominant voicemail is about two out of 10. The Dominant is my favorite personality type for this system because, along with the Influencer, they return our voicemails more often than not.

The voicemail greeting of an Influencer tends to be the longest of the four types. It could even have motivational music on it—you know, "The Eye of the Tiger" or Katy Perry's "Fireworks."

Of course, the word "love" is in the Influencer's greeting: "Love to call you back." "Love to talk with you." The word "sorry" is also very common: "Sorry we missed you." "Sorry I'm away from the phone."

There are two secrets in this voicemail message. First, you *must* use the word "love" in the message that you leave. Second, you must end your voicemail message exactly the way they end their voicemail greeting. Listen and write down notes. The ending usually sounds something like this: "Have a great day!" "Thank you for calling!" or "We appreciate you!" I even have a recording of someone ending their greeting with "Toodle-oo!" You guessed it. I ended my message for them by saying, "Toodle-oo!"

Here is your script for the Influencer.

"Hey, it's me, Dave. I have some exciting news from our office and I would love to share it with you! I'm at 208-123-4567, 208-123-4567." Next is the part where you end the message just like they do: "Remember, it's up to you to have an awesome day!" "Thank you, and have a great day!" or my favorite ending of all time, "Thank you and toodle-oo!"

Note that I left my phone number twice, just in case the Influencer missed it because they were so excited about getting my message.

The reason the Influencer script works so well is this personality is all about being loved. Simply by listening to their work of art—their voicemail greeting—and playing it back to them with your own words, they feel loved and will return your message. This is the place where you can use "love" in your script! If you don't like using the word "love," this is a good way to challenge yourself—20 seconds of insane courage will create incredible results.

THE STEADY TYPE

The Steady personality may be the most difficult to pick up on. However, once you master this technique, you can hear clues right away that tell you to use the Steady voicemail script.

Their voicemail greeting is partially their voice and partially a computer's voice. When we break down the Compliant voicemail, it will be an entirely computer generated voice. However, the Steady uses their voice for part of the greeting and the rest is the computer.

Here is what it sounds like:

The greeting begins with a computer voice. "You have reached the voicemail of . . ." (Here it will change to the person's recorded voice.) "Karen Davis, Clinical Services . . ." (Now it will end with the computer-generated voice.) "At the sound of the tone, please press one to leave a voice message. Press two for human resources. Press three for accounts payable."

Remember, tone and tempo are 93 percent of communication. The spoken word makes up the other seven percent. Focus on using a soft tone with the Steady and speak slowly.

Here is the Steady script:

"Hey, it's me, Dave. I have an idea to enhance your car's performance." (The word "enhance" is key because Steadies do not like change. Focus on the word "enhance.") "I will be available at 10 this morning, at noon, or just after four this afternoon. Our number is 208-123-4567." Give three optional times because a Steady likes to have three choices. Please be slow, soft, and deliberate in your delivery of the voicemail.

THE COMPLIANT TYPE

The Compliant voice greeting is the easiest to pick up on because it is 100 percent computer generated. Like the Steady, the Compliant is about two out of 10 of your calls. Typically, Compliants don't return voicemails unless they know who you are, so this is the only message of the four where you will identify where you're calling from. Keep in mind that the tone and tempo is that of a drum major in a marching band or of a metronome: iambic pentameter. Listen to the tempo and match the beats of the person on the other end of the phone.

After the automated answering machine or the computer generated voice, your script reads:

"Hey, it's me, Dave. I'm calling from GoDaveTester. com. I think it might be important that you call me back. I'm at 208-123-4567, 208-123-4567." Leave the number twice and then hang up.

You probably see some similarities here to the Dominant message. But while you are bold with the Dominant, here you march to a distinct tone and rhythm. Share the phone number twice and provide the client or prospect the name of the company you're calling from.

My mom once changed my grandmother's famous recipe for apple pies. When the pie was baked, we all cut into it thinking it was going to be just like grandma's homemade apple pie. I couldn't wait to taste it! However, when I bit into the pie, it was horrible. I didn't want to hurt her feelings and, lucky for me, Grandma spoke up and said, "What did you do to my pie?" My mother answered, "I changed the recipe to fit how I think it should be done." My grandmother said, "When you don't follow the directions line by line, the pie isn't the same and, in some cases, it's just plain bad." We all agreed. Sorry, Mom. Follow the recipe.

You will be tempted to change my recipe for voice-mails. Please don't do that. I would rather you leave a one minute and thirty second message with the word love in it five times than mess up what I have built here for you.

Trust the recipe. Practice your script and follow the process. This *works*.

Here's a secret tip: If you're not sure what the personality of the greeting is, hang up and call back again. Take the time to figure it out. But note that when you hang up and call back, there is a good chance the client will pick up the phone and say hello. Please don't hang up. The goal of leaving a voicemail is getting them to call you back and say hello.

Remember, the worst time to think of what to say is when it comes out of your mouth. Please practice and *own* your voicemail script.

FEARLESS COMMUNICATION KEY TAKEAWAYS

- The goal of leaving a voicemail is to get a return call. Effective voicemails make customers want to call you back.

- Listen to voicemail recordings and plan what you're going to say based on the personality type.

- Keep voicemails as short as possible. The average voicemail is 65 seconds long. Less is more when it comes to voicemail.

8

The "I Miss You" Letter

When was the last time you wrote an "I miss you" letter?

I'm sure that, if you even write letters at all, it has been many moons. The "I miss you" letter is an excuse to reach out to old clients to tell them you miss them and invite them back into the office again.

According to my research, 93 percent of customers who have had a bad experience with your company will not tell you what happened. In fact, you think you solved the problem, but of those 93 percent that had an issue, nine out of 10 will not return.

Tony Robbins, the great motivational speaker, once taught me, "Nothing happens until the unspoken is said." That couldn't be more accurate in customer care. We focus so much on fixing the issue that we often forget to fix the customer.

This is an incredibly valuable chapter for your business because it's also a way to generate new revenue. The fastest way to grow your business is to ask your current customers to spend more or, in this case, ask former customers to come back again. It costs less to keep customers in your bucket than it does to find new ones.

Here is how we have designed the "I miss you" phone call. When you make this call, it's important to have the heart of a servant and to listen with the intent to understand rather than the intent to respond. Listening and taking notes is the key to the "I miss you" phone call.

When you make any kind of call, you should always have a plan before picking up the phone. It should be written down in front of you. What is the purpose of the call? What is the process of the call, or what script are you going to use? What is the payoff for the call? What has to happen for the call to be successful? Always think of purpose, process, and payoff.

1. Purpose of the call: Generate a new lead

2. Process of the call: Use the "I miss you" letter script

3. Payoff of the call: The old customer is reengaged

When I make this call to someone who has not been back in six to 18 months, I like to have some kind of an offer, such as buy one get one free, a free oil change, no set-up fee, or a free invite to a boot camp. Work with your team to develop the right offer for your business.

When I call the former client, I start with, "Hey, it's me, Dave! Did I catch you at a bad time?" Nine times out of ten they will say no. Then I continue, "I work for a company called Dialing Strangers. Does that ring a bell?" They are more than likely going to say no.

"That's actually the reason I'm calling. We haven't done a very good job staying in touch with you and I just wanted to call you to let you know we miss you."

The former client may say something like, "Okay, who are you?" or "I remember you."

Stick to the script. "Did we do something wrong? What could we have done better?"

Always listen for what is not being said.

The customer should rate their previous experience somewhere between one and five stars. Let's pretend it's a three-star rating this time, which is often the case. It's the kind of situation where you might have just forgotten about the client. You didn't follow up like you should have and took them for granted.

Next, offer the free item and invite them to come to the office. Likewise, if you are mobile, it's an opportunity to go out and see the client.

Again, this is an "I miss you" letter. You screwed up and didn't stay in touch. Use the script "That's not like us. When would you be willing to come back in?"

The quickest way to build business is to ask your current customers to do more business with you and to ask your old clients to come back. I once said to a former customer about coming back, "What is the statute of limitations on you being mad at us?"

Sure, some will say they'll never come back. But others will be more than happy to give you a second chance.

Master the "I miss you" letter today.

- "Hey, it's me, Dave! Did I catch you at a bad time? I work for a company called Dialing Strangers. Does that ring a bell?"

- "We haven't done a very good job staying in touch with you and I just wanted to call you to let you know we miss you."

- "Did we do something wrong? What could we have done better?"

- Listen for what is not being said.

- "That's not like us. When would you be willing to come back in?"

FEARLESS COMMUNICATION KEY TAKEAWAYS

- The fastest way to grow your business is to ask your current customers to spend more or ask former customers to come back again.

- Listen with the intent to understand rather than the intent to respond.

- You should always have a plan for the call written down in front of you before picking up the phone.

9

Delivering Bad News

I hate to admit this.

When I was in high school, I wasn't always the best student. In fact, sometimes I was the opposite.

Don't misunderstand me. My grades were solid. It's just that young Mr. Tester—that's what my teachers called me when I was in trouble—liked to talk during class. And I didn't just like to talk. Oh no, I liked to talk *a lot*.

I looked at it as an opportunity to practice for my broadcasting career. Most of my instructors were not amused. In fact, my economics teacher was so dismayed by my talking during class that he threatened to flunk me. Unfortunately, that meant I would not be graduating from high school during my senior year.

"What? I have an A and you're going to flunk me?" I questioned him, completely dumbfounded by his audacity.

"Damn straight, Mr. Tester!"

Ouch. Mr. McFarland sent me home with a "poor work" slip. A parent needed to sign it, and I remember my mom telling me, "Your dad will have to sign this, DJ."

Inflammatory names like "Mr. Tester" and initials like "DJ" (David Jon) were never a good sign, even coming from my mother. Although the real Mr. (Dr.) Tester (my dad) was busy working as a veterinarian, my mom assured me that he would make time to sign this pink "poor work" slip. Why did it have to be pink?

Everyone in school knew I was in trouble for talking. I took all of the optional 30 days to get my required signature. I assure you that I did quit talking in class. However, Dr. Tester had not signed the pink slip yet. Eventually I did muster up the courage to give the slip to my dad and await my punishment. To my surprise, however, Dad just laughed when he saw it and said, "Yes, the same thing happened to me." In fact, he added, "Please do me a favor and stop talking in class if you want to go to college. In the future, why don't you tell me the bad news early, *before* I hear it from someone else?"

You guessed it: that "someone else" was a client of my dad's whose name just happened to be Mr. McFarland.

There are two lessons here. First, bad news is not like wine—it doesn't get better with time. I should have delivered the bad news to my dad right away and dealt with the cards however they might have fallen, which, as it turned out, was not so bad.

The second lesson is to deliver bad news before the recipient hears it from someone else. I guess no one, not even my dad, likes surprises of this nature. By the way, I did pass the class and graduated that spring. Thank you, Mr. McFarland, for teaching me these principles of delivering bad news.

Before we dive into the script, I want you to think about your business and what kind of bad news you might have to deliver. Many people are afraid the client on the phone will be mad at them. We can't always control the fear of inbound calls, but we *can* control the fear of outbound calls when we have to deliver bad news. I'm going to help you with a system that can be very empowering, both for the client and for you.

First, I want you to list three to six potential bad news deliveries that you sometimes have to make in your business. I will lead off with a few common bad news items that are bound to happen in just about every business.

1. The promised service will not be completed on time.

2. The procedure is going to cost more money than originally quoted to the customer.

3. Your company made a mistake.

4. There was a mix-up in communication.

I want you and your team to list some bad news items you have had to deal with or fear that you might have to face.

I've discovered that most deliveries of bad news are similar, no matter the industry. The sick feeling in your stomach is also the same. "What if they're mad at me?" "What if they give us a bad review?" "What if the client leaves us?" And, the worst fear of all is "What if I lose my job over this?"

Always remember this, even if the client doesn't believe it: you didn't wake up this morning and decide, "I'm going to rip off my customer and change the quote" or "I'm going to finish the job late just for fun!" Sometimes life just happens. You need to have a plan to deliver bad news to your customers on those hopefully rare occasions.

The first element of delivering bad news is to remind yourself that this is about the problem, not the person. It is very similar to the Volcano Theory. Your mission is to focus on the problem and make an agreement with the customer ahead of time.

Part of the sales and fulfillment process for my own clients is asking the question, "What if we have to deliver bad news to you?" Honesty is always the best policy. "We try our best, but we don't always *do* our best." You can even ask your clients up front, "How should I deliver bad news to you?"

If this is part of your system from the beginning, I can assure you that your customers will grow to view you as a trusted advisor rather than as a salesperson or vendor. Some of my clients ask me, "Why would you want to bring up bad news?" I bring up bad news early because that's what my clients have told me they want.

Here is how it often plays out in real time when my clients answer this question up front: "Yes, I understand that bad news is going to come our way in the building process. Please let me know right away with a phone call and also bring me a plan to deal with it so we can move forward."

Another client said to me, "Will you be mad at me when I give you bad news?" I might be mad for a minute, but I will get over it and we will get on with solving the issue. "If you're going to be late on the finish time, let me know so I don't bring in product too early and it costs us all a lot more money than it should."

Delivering bad news should be like delivering good news. I admit that giving my dad a report card with an A was a lot more fun than giving him the "poor work" slip, but carrying that angst around with me in my churning stomach for 30 days was definitely *not* healthy. Afterward, I understood. Later, in college, there was more bad news to deliver to my dad. I was smart about it because we'd had the discussion before. I gave him the bad news early, and always before he heard it from someone else. I don't think Dad was mad at me, but he was unhappy with the situation. More importantly, he was always just happy that I was okay, even if my choices or priorities were disappointing to him.

I know for a company it may seem like the issue at hand is the most important thing in the world and that your disgruntled client will change the rotation of the world itself. That is not the case. Always put it in perspective.

The number one takeaway from this chapter is to stop using the word "sorry" when you deliver bad news. Try listening throughout your day to how many people tell you they are sorry. It's become an almost robotic response that means nothing. I hear "sorry" all the time. It's no longer good enough to simply be sorry.

Instead, use the statement, "That's not like us!" Follow up with "We always try our best, but we don't always *do* our best. In this case, we are better than that!" By using this line, you have answered many questions in the client's mind. Let me remind you, please do *not* be sorry. Be proactive and let them know that this disappointing performance is not characteristic of you and your business.

The most difficult element of this process is resisting the temptation to try to read the mind of your client. Delivering bad news always leads the person who has to deliver it to think, "If it were me, I would be mad." Remember this: it is not about *you*. It is about *them,* and you should always treat the customer how they want to be treated. In this case, deliver the news how *they* want it to be delivered.

The foundation for all my training is the DISC personality types. If you have a customer retention system or a customer database, you should always have the personality type of the customer listed in the file.

The Dominant customer is simply concerned. They do not want to be taken advantage of, and they always want to win. Make sure that you deliver the news early in your relationship so as not to take advantage of the customer. Work to build a solution where the client can feel like it's truly a win for them.

The Influencer is worried about being loved. This is challenging because this personality can sometimes mislead us to think they are okay with the bad news. I always let this personality type know that we will still be friends no matter what they need to tell me. Give them permission to vent.

The Steady personality is worried about change. This could be a change in their order or a change of plans. Think of what you are doing to resolve the issue as an *enhancement* rather than a change. Always give this personality type three options for what can be done to fix the bad news. Focus on being quiet and give them the time to think. Follow up this thoughtful time with a question like "Can you tell me what you are thinking?" Give them room to breathe.

The Compliant personality type just wants to make sure you follow the rules and stick to the facts. Most of this bad news work can be done via email with them. Email is my least favorite way of communicating. However, it is what they typically prefer. Please don't criticize or question any decision they have made in the process. Allow them to be correct and always stick with facts rather than feelings.

You can begin to understand why it is vital to keep track of personality types in your database. I am happy to come in for a full day and explain how it works and the magic of the platinum rule: treating people how they want to be treated.

There are a few other elements to consider when delivering bad news. Please do not throw teammates or colleagues under the proverbial bus. This type of response might sound like "They didn't know what they were doing," or "He shouldn't have fixed it that way." The worst response of all is "It's not my fault."

When I make live customer care calls for clients delivering bad news, I will often add the statement, "I take full responsibility." This eliminates all of the emotion that is stirred up by the question "Who's fault is it, anyway?" Once I take responsibility, I can begin to lay out the vision of what has to happen to provide a solution.

The definition of courage is putting your fear aside and focusing on the job at hand. Most of the bad news isn't as bad as we think, but we let it fester into some incredible story in our own heads until we're certain it has a terrible ending.

Follow your script. Depending on the size of the job or service, you can ask before the sale or in the fulfillment process, "In the unlikely event that we have to deliver bad news, how do you prefer that I deliver it to you?"

Please do your best not to lead your conversation with, "I've got some really bad news for you," or "We have a *bit* of a problem." Focus on your script and how the customer prefers the news to be delivered. Tell them as early as possible and before they hear it from someone else.

Do you remember the phrase to use if the conversation gets too heated? "Ma'am, you're not mad at me, are you?" Nine times out of ten, they will back off and start over.

As I used to tell my daughter when she was in middle school and we got off on the wrong foot first thing in the morning,

"Clare, let's go back and start the day over again." This technique works and allows you to start over.

For the one time in ten when the customer is still mad at you, let me remind you that you have not been hired to take any kind of customer abuse. Reach out to your supervisor or the owner and hand the client off to them. You are not here to be hurt. You are here to help.

Get the bad news over with as quickly as possible. In hindsight, I know I shouldn't have waited 30 days to give my dad the "poor work" slip.

Remember, no mind-reading, and always keep in mind that bad news is not like wine—it does not get better with time.

- "That's not like us."
- "How should I deliver bad news to you?"
- "We try our best, but we don't always *do* our best."
- "I'm in charge of the training here, and I take full responsibility for not following up with you."
- "Are you mad at me?"
- "In the unlikely event that we have to deliver bad news, how do you prefer that I deliver it to you?"
- Give the news early.
- Give the news before they hear it from someone else.
- Provide three solutions: Good, better, and best.

FEARLESS COMMUNICATION KEY TAKEAWAYS

- Bad news is not like wine—it doesn't get better with time.

- Deliver bad news before the recipient hears it from someone else.

- Stop using the word "sorry" when you deliver bad news. It's become an almost robotic response that means nothing. It's no longer good enough to simply be sorry. Instead, focus on using "That's not like us."

10

What If They Ask a Question and I Don't Know the Answer?

When I answered the phone for my dad, I was worried that a client might be upset, but an even greater fear was a customer asking me a question I didn't know the answer to.

I viewed myself as considerably smarter than the average sixth grader at the time. However, I had no idea how to treat a horse with colic, a dog with porcupine quills, or a cow that was calving. No matter my level of knowledge, I learned quickly that I would be asked many questions that I wouldn't know the answer to. As a human being, you will inevitably find yourself in the same situation. No one can know everything, especially in the rapidly changing business environment of the twenty-first century. Consequently, this fear of the unknown has the potential to render anyone ineffective if they let it.

I want you to understand there is no reason to fear situations where a client asks you a question that you don't know the answer to. In fact, such situations are opportunities to increase your value and your brand. With my technique of asking a question in response to a question, you'll discover what your clients and customers are really looking for.

Think about visiting your doctor for a moment. If you're like most people, you don't go in just because it's time to get an annual physical. More often than not, there is an ailment or symptom that has prompted you to finally invest the time and effort to make an appointment. If the doctor just performs a physical but fails to ask you any questions, the doctor will likely miss the issue entirely.

The number one question that potential clients ask is "How much is it?"

Yes, this is the dreaded price question that can cause the most battle-hardened salesperson to break into a cold sweat. Many professionals have been coached not to give out prices. However, if you grew up in a house like I did, when your mom or dad asked you a question, you answered it. You answered it the first time—or else.

It sounded something like this: "Young man, I asked you a question and I expect an answer." Does that sound at all familiar to you? I made sure to always have an answer.

Too many sales coaches try to put Mom and Dad's principles out to pasture. But Mom and Dad knew what they were talking about. Imagine what they might say in response.

"That's a great question. Why are you asking that?"

These two simple sentences can make life a lot easier for you on the phone if you master the technique.

It goes something like this: The son comes home from junior high school football practice and asks his mom, "What's for dinner?" Mom, of course, knows this is code for "I don't like what you are making. Can we go out for tacos instead?"

Mom is tired of this routine and says, "No snacking. I've worked on dinner all afternoon and you're not going to spoil it."

Do you remember the question behind the question? "Mom, I would like to invite friends over for dinner. Do we have enough for all of them to eat here with us?"

Our challenge as sales professionals is to resist the urge to jump to conclusions. For example, when a potential client asks, "How much is it?" we tend to think they are price shopping. In the example, Mom assumes that her growing boy just doesn't like what she's cooking. It's so easy to miss the *actual* question.

Let's play out the conversation between mother and son but using my technique this time around.

"Mom, what's for dinner tonight?"

Mom is now going to ask a question in response to a question. "That is a great question, son. Your dad just asked me the same thing. Why are you asking?"

This shrewd move on Mom's part frees up her son to ask the *real* question that he wanted to lead with all along.

"Trevor and Conner's parents are out of town and I wanted to invite them over for dinner. Do you have enough for them to join us?"

As you follow my system and scripts, you'll begin to understand the question behind the question and how you can find out what people are *really* asking.

You don't need to have all of the answers. You just need to ask the right questions.

My favorite example of how this often plays out is when someone asks the simple question, "What's in a hot dog?" I grew up in the West and a rite of passage was my grandfather telling me all of the bad stuff that was used to make hot dogs. Trust me, if you own a hotdog stand and someone asks that question, don't simply answer it. If you do, *no one* will purchase your product. You will go broke.

I'm not asking you to mislead, lie, or cheat. Simply use a clarifying question. When someone asks you what is in a hot dog, follow up by saying, "That's a great question. I get asked that a lot. Why are you asking it?"

Now the prospect can ask me the *real* question: "Do you have a vegan hot dog?"

Now the answer becomes, "Absolutely, we do! How many would you like?"

Or perhaps the customer is trying to cut back on carbs. "I was wondering, could we get a hot dog without a bun?"

"Absolutely, you can!"

If you merely answered the question at face value—"What are the ingredients in a hot dog?"—you can bet both of these potential customers would have left for life.

Now you may ask, "What if they really want to know what is in a hot dog?" Don't worry, the process works the same way.

Again, I always respond with a question. "Great question. You must be asking me for a reason."

"Because I want to know what is in a hot dog!"

Answer the question and tell them the ingredients in a hot dog, simple as that.

This could be a sincere question from a genuinely curious person or it could just be taking a while to get to the *real* question. In order to determine this, follow up with a question such as, "It sounds like maybe you've had a bad experience with hot dogs in the past?"

Remember the purpose of what we're trying to accomplish. You're learning to focus on booking an appointment. Your job is not to educate the client or the prospect; it is to book the appointment. If you educate the prospect or talk too much, you will walk your way out of the sale and sabotage your own success by answering unasked questions, thereby opening a new hole in your lead bucket that the client or prospect may slip through.

An example was when I was once asked by a potential client if our company worked on weekends. At first, I wanted to tell them that we work 24/7, 365 days a year. However, I followed my own system and ended up saving the day.

"Great question, sir! You must be asking me that question for a reason." Note I did not answer a question that was unasked.

He said, "Dave, we are Seventh Day Adventists and our sabbath is Friday night and Saturday. We do not want anyone working at our location on our sabbath."

My response was, "Absolutely, we do not work on those days at your home."

Now comes the question you cannot avoid. Believe it or not, there will one day be a question that you do not have the answer to. The main reason I'm teaching you this technique is to keep you off of the price question. Most people ask about price because we have trained them to ask the price. The other reason people ask for the price is to keep you from over-talking. Avoid saying things like "If it were me, this is what I would do." Please never use that statement, even if the prospect asks you for advice.

You won't be able to avoid the question you don't know the answer to. When this fateful moment finally comes, simply say, "I don't know the answer." However, the story does *not* stop here! Tell them you will find out the answer to their question and call them back.

With the system and the scripts that I have created for you, you will never have to wing it again or make things up. The worst time to think of something to say is when it comes out of your mouth. Truly own the script.

Many people don't like scripts because they "sound too scripted."

My response is "Does an actor sound scripted?" No, because they take that script and they *own* it. If actors in plays or movies didn't have scripts to follow, it would be a complete disaster. Great actors never say, "I sound too scripted," or "I've been doing this for a long time, and I know the audience can tell I sound scripted." Better yet, they don't say, "I can just go off the cuff." Not even improvisational comedians truly go off the cuff. They have guidelines and landing marks to stick to so the production sounds ad lib, even though it is scripted flawlessly.

The homework for this chapter is to practice the single line you must master at home. When your spouse, kids, or parents ask you a question, get in the habit of saying, "That is a great question. You must be asking me that for a reason." Not only will this change the dynamics in your relationships, but you will also discover what the question behind the question is. Just like the mom discovered when her son asked what was for dinner, it may have nothing to do with your assumption about it.

Practice these techniques on friends and family members, but do not practice on customers and prospects. That's called sales malpractice.

- "That's a great question. Why are you asking?"
- If you don't know the answer, simply say, "I don't know. But I will find out and call you back."

FEARLESS COMMUNICATION KEY TAKEAWAYS

- A client asking you a question you don't know the answer to is not scary—it's an opportunity to increase your value and your brand.

- Remember to ask a question in response to a question: "That's a great question. Why are you asking that?"

- Own your scripts. Don't practice on clients and prospects. Practice them on family and friends instead.

Dave's Secret Sauce

I have a friend who happens to be one of the greatest sales copywriters in the world. He taught me to create great headlines. His name is Ray Edwards. One of the techniques Ray uses is called the "secret file." Sounds pretty compelling, right?

As I spent more time with Ray, I discovered that the secret file wasn't really so secret. It was just smart. It was a comprehensive look at all the tools we had just learned about copywriting. In this case, my secret file is a review of all that we've discovered in this book.

I tell the same thing to my students, business owners, customer service representatives, sales team members, and just about anyone else who will listen to me: you have access to all of my tools. It's like taking food at a buffet. Take all that you need, but be sure to use all that you take. Here is the secret file:

- "It's a great day at our business! This is Dave. How may I help you?"
- "Remind me of your name . . ."
- "Real quick, how do I spell your last name?"
- "In case we get disconnected, your cell phone number is . . . ?" Lead with your local area code. Here in Idaho I would say 208. When asking for an email address, the statement works the same way. Instead of using an area code, I use Gmail.com and the first name. "Real quick, your email address is dave@gmail. com?" Typically, the prospect will respond, "No, but you're close. It's testerbroadcaster@gmail.com."
- "Shall I book that in pen or in pencil?"
- "You don't see anything between now and then that would keep you from making this appointment, do you? Friday is the lead-in to Labor Day."
- "Do I have your word?"
- "Off the record, can you tell me what is going on?"
- "It sounds like you would be willing to give me a five-star Google review?"
- "I don't know how you feel, but I do understand. I'm taking notes. Is that okay?"
- "Tell me more."
- "I get the feeling I've done something to offend you. Is it just me, or is that the case?"
- "Would it make sense for me to invite you in?"

- "Would it make sense for you to invite us into your home to take a look at the furnace?"
- "Hey, it's me, Dave. I think it's important you call me back: 208-123-4567." Hang up.
- "I'm calling to apologize. I was supposed to follow up and I didn't. You're not upset at me, are you?"
- "That's not like us. I take full responsibility."
- "We always try our best, but we don't always *do* our best."
- "Tell me more." Did I already tell you that you can use this technique many times during the same call? Please, no sound effects. Just listen and take great notes.
- "How do you like bad news to be delivered?"
- "Hey, it's me, Dave. Did I catch you at a bad time?"
- "That's a great question. I get asked that a lot. You must be asking me for a reason?"
- "I get the feeling you've had a bad experience."
- "Let me repeat what I'm hearing you say just to make sure we're on the same page."
- No mind reading!
- Never answer unasked questions.
- "What *should* have happened?"
- "What would you like to see happen next?"
- "You're not mad at me, are you?"
- "How did you hear about us? On Google? Oh, what did Google say?"

- Everyone believes the issue they have at the moment is the most important one in the world. It may well be. However, to clarify, we can simply ask, "Is this issue a 911?" If they say yes, move on to finding a solution right away. We've found that nine times out of ten, it's important, but not a 911. I discovered this tool from my daughter telling me she is sick and may need to go see the doctor. I said to her, "Let's go to the emergency room right now!" She then replied, "It's not that bad, Dad." And remember, if it truly *is* that bad, we move to the emergency room right away!

Acknowledgments

"When you learn, teach. When you get, give."
— **Maya Angelou**

My mom used to say, "Just tell DJ (that's me) it can't be done, and he'll find a way to do it." Thank you, Mom, for challenging me.

My high school English teacher told me, "You will never graduate from college, and there is no way you will write a book." At least, that is how I heard it in my mind. After Mrs. Johnson made that statement, things changed. First came college, then some essays, and eventually my first book, *Dialing Strangers*. Mrs. Johnson, I know you just wanted me to be all I could be. Thank you.

So many clients, prospects, friends, and family members have contributed in one way or another to help put the words on the page. I cannot thank you enough.

My assistant, Joelle, was the compass that kept this book (and me) on track. Thank you for getting this project over the finish line.

Thank you, Aloha Publishing, for being a great partner in what we are hoping will be the first of many books published together.

Thank you, Dr. Derrick Nelson, DVM, in Ft. Worth, for being the first to implement our program from chapter 1 through chapter 10 and proving that it works just like magic.

Thank you to Mike and Nancy Sharp, my second family. Jeff Cox, thank you for allowing me to create training programs based on *Fearless Communication* for your team, clients, and leads. Tom Beeles, thank you for continuing to use my inbound and outbound training systems. Thank you to Shaun Buck, Lo, Amanda, and the team—who prove every day that *Fearless Communication* works, and that practice does make perfect.

A special thank you to the four C's: Claudia, Carson, Clare, and Christ.

About the Author

The secret to Dave Tester's coaching, consulting, and speaking success comes from his extensive background in sports journalism and coaching hundreds of business clients. A dedicated student of the great trainers, Dave has developed a tried-and-true system for networking and deal-making that positively changes how companies sell products and services.

Dave has owned or operated nearly 25 radio stations and personally trained and coached employees to unprecedented levels—transforming struggling companies into market leaders. Dave has served as a sports anchor for Fox TV Sports, ESPN, CNN, ABC, and CBS, where he won multiple awards for his unique brand of storytelling and gripping play-by-play calls.

I chose the photo to the right because of the words behind my friend, Coby Baker, and I. The photo forces you to ask a question: "Train your . . . what?" If you know anything about me, you can probably guess what that last word is. "Train Your Mind."

I bring this up because I believe inherently in the power of the human mind. Inside every single human being is a mind capable of infinite things: Infinite good. Infinite growth. Infinite success. Everything that I do as an author, speaker, trainer, and coach is motivated by a genuine desire to see every human being tap into their innate potential. In order to do this, however, the mind has to be trained.

That's where I can help.

Fearless Communication is just one part of what I can do to help train your mind and those of your team for success. Because this is my mission, I have a nearly endless supply of practical tools for your success. By empowering leaders and employees alike to overcome fears, channel potential, and build skills, I've been able to experience the joy of seeing hundreds of professionals exceed their own expectations. I'd love to visit with you about the possibilities.

Made in the USA
Monee, IL
14 August 2021